RILKE'S BOOK OF HOURS

Translated by

ANITA BARROWS

and

JOANNA MACY

RIVERHEAD BOOKS

NEW YORK

1996

RILKE'S
BOOK OF
HOURS

LOVE POEMS TO GOD

RIVERHEAD BOOKS
a division of G. P. Putnam's Sons
Publishers Since 1838
200 Madison Avenue
New York, NY 10016

Library of Congress Cataloging-in-Publication Data

Rilke, Rainer Maria, 1875–1926.
[Stundenbuch.   English]
Rilke's book of hours: love poems to God/
translated by Anita Barrows and Joanna Macy.
p.   cm.
ISBN 1-57322-033-7
I. Barrows, Anita.   II. Macy, Joanna, date.   III. Title.
PT2635.I65S725   1996   95-49149 CIP
831′.912—dc20

Printed in the United States of America
1   3   5   7   9   10   8   6   4   2

This book is printed on acid-free paper. ∞

BOOK DESIGN BY MARYSARAH QUINN

CONTENTS

PREFACE BY JOANNA MACY

1

PREFACE BY ANITA BARROWS

9

INTRODUCTION

17

NOTES ON THE TRANSLATION

35

THE BOOK OF A MONASTIC LIFE

45

THE BOOK OF PILGRIMAGE

93

THE BOOK OF POVERTY AND DEATH

125

COMMENTARY

149

PREFACE

JOANNA MACY

For almost forty years, since the winter's day I found it on a table in a Munich bookstore, Rainer Maria Rilke's *Book of Hours* has been a cherished companion. It is the original Insel Verlag edition, clothbound, with Gothic script on soft rag paper, and on the cover the logo of the three-jetted fountain the poet designed. This pocket-size volume has traveled with me across the spiritual landscapes of my life—from the rubble of a once sturdy faith in church and God, into the streets of political activism, and into the Buddhafields of South and Central Asia.

The first poem I recall reading was as exhilarating to me as the fresh cold alpine wind off the slopes I loved to ski.

> I live my life in widening circles
> that reach out across the world.
> I may not ever complete the last one,
> but I give myself to it.
>
> I circle around God, that primordial tower.
> I have been circling for thousands of years,
> and I still don't know: am I a falcon,
> a storm, or a great song?   I, 2

I felt a sense of release, as if I had been let out of a cage I had not known I was in. Rilke's images lent some pattern, even meaning, to a life I thought had failed in its spiritual vocation. Once I had imagined that my journey would be like the Pilgrim's Progress, where each adventure brings the hero closer to the heavenly city, but the Christian God with whom I had been intoxicated in my teenage years did not survive the theological studies I undertook to serve him (and it was a him). When I turned outward, angry and heartsick, to political affairs, I found that I was a failure as an atheist, too, for I could not cure myself of praying to a God I no longer believed in.

Now those same lines, read on a snow-packed Munich street, shed a new light on the patchwork my life had become—marriage, motherhood, abandoned government career, assortment of jobs, studies in art and language. Perhaps, after all, some unknowable center held me in orbit. Rilke reminded me that if my spiritual appetite was greater than the tedious, cramped theorizing of the theologians, so was God. I could almost feel again the sense of belonging and purpose that I thought I had forfeited.

The Book of Hours came with me to Asia, eight years later, when I went to live in India, with my young family and the Peace Corps. There, through work with Tibetan refugees, Buddhism entered my life and brought a sense of ease and strength in the patterns it revealed for structuring experience—patterns that seemed familiar. Rilke in

The Book of Hours had expressed the sacred in terms and images I now found central to Buddhist teachings, concepts such as "law" and "way" (*"du sanftestes Gesetz . . ."*), and images of wheel and net ("You are a wheel at which I stand"; "you dark net threading through us").

When I undertook meditative practice, I did not feel the divine presence, the encompassing Other to be held and supported by, that was there for the young Rilke.

> Don't you sense me, ready to break
> into being at your touch?   I, 19

But gradually over time, as the mind relaxed, capacities bred by my earlier Christian experience resurfaced and infused my understanding of Buddhism. The presence that I became aware of, around and within me, is apprehended through an act of rapt, silent attention, both passive and probing, like sonar. And what the presence seems to *be* is the web itself, the thrumming relationality of all things.

Rilke's recognition of the reciprocal nature of our relationship to God and to life itself is a poetic and profoundly personal complement to the Buddha's central doctrine of dependent co-arising, which asserts the radical interdependence at the core of existence. Although fascinating, it was too often abstract—so I loved reading again: "What will you do, God, when I die?" (I, 36).

This sense of reciprocity nourished my engagement in

work for social change, and was fed by it in turn. There came a time in the middle and late 1970s when the enormity of what I was discovering as an environmental activist—especially about the widespread, long-term, devastating effects of nuclear waste—broke through my defenses. I struggled simply to take in what was happening to our world, and to sustain the gaze long enough to be of use. Rilke's unwhining acceptance of the fact that, yes, a world can die, strengthened me with its straightforwardness and lack of self-pity.

I found that many of my colleagues and fellow citizens were silently suffering and suppressing a similar anguish. Buddhist teachings and my Judeo-Christian roots helped me understand this pain for the world. Rilke helped, too.

> You are not surprised at the force of the storm—
> you have seen it growing. . . .

> Now you must go out into your heart
> as onto a vast plain. Now
> the immense loneliness begins. . . .

> Through the empty branches the sky remains.
> It is what you have.   II, 1

Those lines murmured like mantras in my mind. I felt Rilke helping me face this time of terror and promise, as I moved out into the public arena with a form of group work based explicitly on the extent and depth of our social despair.

> Lord, the great cities are lost and rotting.
> Their time is running out.   III, 4

The work I offered helps people overcome denial about the condition of our world. By understanding and embracing their despair, they come to their senses again and transform the despair itself into strong, connective energy.

That your world is in agony is no reason to turn your back on it, or to try to escape into private "spiritual" pursuits. Rilke reminded me that I had the strength and courage to walk out into the world as into my own heart, and to "love the things / as no one has thought to love them" (I, 61).

My own stubborn, wild love for the world was summoned, and I learned to recognize it in others, too, in workshops and strategy sessions of the peace and environmental movements. Rilke confirmed my sense of a deep passion at the core of life itself which I could come home to, the way sheep come home at nightfall, "the dark bridge thudding" (I, 40). I could die into that passion, as into a lover's arms, trusting its ongoingness and its vast sufficient intelligence.

With Rilke I learned to recognize that intelligence—the "play of the powers"—in the simplest of things, to take comfort in the texture of bark, the acorn's gleaming body, the leaping squirrel. The poet's images of web and wheel, of root and branch, reminded me how the things connect, in interwoven patterns and mutual belonging.

Your wholeness cascades into many shapes.
You run like a herd of luminous deer
and I am dark, I am forest.   I, 45

Rilke never said that the path to political empowerment lay through darkness, he just said God was there. But he bolstered my conviction that we must go that way in order to break out of denial and let the "play of the powers," the intelligence of life, work through us, so we can learn again to live simply, in kinship with creation.

Naturally, over the years, I wanted to share *The Book of Hours* with my friends. I searched in vain for English translations that conveyed their brave, luminous simplicity. Sometimes, in spells of sadness or dryness, when I wanted to enter the poems more deeply, I tried my hand at translating them myself. I knew what I was seeking, but I was frustrated by my attempt to hold on to meter and rhyme, which made my efforts in English sound trite.

Then, in 1993, I began again, with my friend Anita

Barrows, an accomplished poet. We started idly, just for the pleasure of it, with a handful of poems that had become most familiar to me. We had no idea that we had embarked on a book, and on one of the most joyous adventures of our lives.

PREFACE

ANITA BARROWS

I knew nothing of the poems in Rilke's *Book of Hours* until
the evening in May 1993 when Joanna Macy read to me,
in German, the two that would initiate our work, "What
will you do, God, when I die?" and "You are not surprised
at the force of the storm." The first, in the affirmation of
God's need for us, seemed very close to a thought that had
accompanied me in childhood. Brought up as I was in a
highly patriarchal Jewish family—both my grandfathers
had been Orthodox rabbis, one in Poland and the other in
Russia—I was steeped in an image of a God who was
anything but dependent. Jealous, hot-tempered, the Yah-
weh I intuited from those around me was a huge, remote
eye in the sky, watching and waiting for us to falter and fail
him.

What could I feel except fear before such a punitive
God? And yet one Saturday in autumn when I was about
six, trailing after my father on the walk home from syna-
gogue, I understood something new about God. There on
the boulevard, amid the noise and bustle of Brooklyn, was
this delicious mulching smell, this crispness, this crackling
noise of dry red and yellow leaves. The smell awakened
me after the morning spent in the dim, drafty synagogue,

9

where I had to sit upstairs listening to the men chanting below in a language I did not understand. *God made these leaves, this smell*, I said to myself; and suddenly it occurred to me that God created the world because he was lonely. He needed it—needed the ripeness of autumn, the bright air, the sunlight making patterns on the sidewalk through linden leaves that were yet unfallen. God had created all this, and us as well, to keep him company. That far, chilly place where he lived had felt empty to him without our world. The idea seemed so blasphemous to me that I dared not speak it, but I found it both exciting and comforting.

Rilke's poem of the great oncoming storm spoke to me of the repeated moments in my life when I had departed from what was known and familiar—a place, a group, a belief, a work—to follow something that compelled me from what seemed a place of deep inner knowing. "Now you must go out into your heart / as onto a vast plain," Rilke wrote.

I had left the synagogue at sixteen in search of something that felt more akin to the God revealed to me under the linden leaves, and less like the father "in king's robes," with "scepter and crown," as Rilke describes the images of God he, too, resisted. Coming west from New York at nineteen, I experienced in the vast, dramatic geography of California the same awe I had felt in the presence of Yahweh, with none of the remoteness. Nature became what was holy for me: the silence of redwoods, the granite peaks of the northern Sierra, the desert. For a long time I did not want to speak about God.

Then, during my graduate student days, my study of medieval Italian literature, especially Dante, drew me to Catholicism, with its incarnate God who loved and suffered humanly. I took instruction in the Church and was baptized. Week after week I received the Eucharist and found great joy in it; but I could not get over feeling like an impostor. My Jewishness would not let me give myself fully to Christian forms and rituals, and anyway, it was the spare medieval monastery I longed for and not the institutional church. After a time I returned to a meditative practice I had been doing on and off for years, without naming it religion; and eventually it was Buddhism that I embraced.

In the spring of 1993, when Joanna and I began working with *The Book of Hours*, I was completing a long poem of my own, which I called *A Record*. I was weaving together images from the Jewish Holocaust with images of the suffering of other peoples and species, the suffering of our earth. The poem was a statement of a passionate understanding that had been developing in me of the interconnectedness of all these forms of suffering. I did not intend to trivialize any particular suffering by setting it alongside others; but some of my Jewish poet friends criticized the poem for doing just that. How could I speak of the dying of frogs and the incineration of Jews in the same breath? Inner voices judged me as well; as a Jewish child born only two years after the liberation of the concentration camps, I was continually told of the atrocities of Nazi Germany. Was I diminishing my people's pain by placing it in context with other pain? And yet I knew, from the ways in which my heart kept breaking over the dying of frogs, the drying up of riverbeds, the blight on the leaves of the trees I loved, that for these, too, a holocaust was occurring, and I had no choice but to name it.

Rilke's summons to the journey into his own heart helped me find the courage to continue writing *A Record*. It helped me, as well, to put into perspective my own doubt about what I was doing and how my friends and colleagues might judge it.

> Be modest now, like a thing
> ripened until it is real,
> so that he who began it all
> can feel you when he reaches for you.   II, 1

What a relief to see myself simply, as Rilke urges, as one bit of God's creation: not as Jewish or Catholic or Buddhist, not as a poet with such-and-such background or reputation—no more important than a branch, a stone, or a drop of water. Rilke's sense of a God who could reach for me in my barest simplicity—in my most "real" and "ripened" self—comforted me.

Reading Rilke again also brought back to me my own beginnings as a poet. In 1964, when I was seventeen, I was invited to spend a week on Cape Cod with a friend whose parents were German. On the long drive up from New York, my friend's father, a writer, recited by heart one after another of Rilke's *Sonnets to Orpheus*—first in German, then in his own elegant impromptu translation. Imagine the fire kindled in me! When, months later, I tentatively brought to my friend's Manhattan apartment a notebook filled with sonnets of my own, her father's first response after reading them was to go to his shelf and pull out a copy of Rilke's *Letters to a Young Poet*. "If you are going to be a poet you must read Rilke," he told me, and gave me the volume to keep. "Rilke is the poet's poet." The letters went everywhere with me for years, along with *The Notebooks of Malte Laurids Brigge*, which I read shortly afterward. It would not be an exaggeration to say that those two books shaped and concentrated for me my vocation as a poet; and when I signed up for a German class in my second year of college, it was with the express purpose of reading Rilke in the original.

When Joanna and I started working—or, actually, playing—with those first two poems, I had not translated anything for a long time, even though I had worked professionally as a translator for ten years before I trained as a psychologist. On my early-morning walks in those weeks after we began, I found myself obsessively turning phrases in my head, and remembered the joy I had experienced in translation—different from the act of writing my own poetry, yet similar. This playful experiment with Rilke's early poems was answering some very deep longing within me. It was a complex longing, born of delight in language, yes, but also of the isolation of being a poet— isolation precisely in moments of the greatest fulfillment my life knew. To share this process, this intimate space, with another person seemed an incredible privilege. It made me quiver with happiness, and also a little apprehension.

Apprehension quickly yielded to the sheer energy of exploration, as Joanna and I allowed these poems to reveal their meanings to us. I discovered yet deeper resonances between them and the most pervasive themes of my life. Rilke's love for things of this world, his insistence that they, we, are what is sacred, his capacity to see the holy in the ordinary—all these have continued to inform my own poetry for thirty years.

> I know that nothing has ever been real
> without my beholding it.
> All becoming has needed me.
> My looking ripens things
> and they come toward me, to meet and be met.   I, 1

A person (or a thing) comes to exist by being met in the most authentic way by another. My practice of psychotherapy has been deeply informed by the Jungian principle of reciprocal individuation, which means that a deep and loving encounter is what generates development.

How close this is to Rilke's declaration that our greatest summons is really to see the things of this world.

We *are* because we are seen; we *are* because we are loved. The world *is* because it is beheld and loved into being. On a silent retreat, while watching a line of ants traveling up a hillside, words came to me that I would repeat again and again in my mind: *I am in the world to love the world*. I knew, standing there in the parched summer grasses, how deeply the poems of *The Book of Hours* had already penetrated my being, speaking to me as instructions for living.

INTRODUCTION

Rilke wrote the poems that make up *The Book of Hours*
(*Das Stundenbuch*) in three brief, intense periods of inspi-
ration between 1899 and 1903. When he began, he was
twenty-three years old and had already published three
volumes of poetry. By the time *The Book of Hours* was
published in December 1905, Rilke had written several of
the works for which he is best known, including *The Lay of
the Love and Death of Cornet Christopher Rilke* and a series of
letters to Franz Kappus, which would be collected under
the title *Letters to a Young Poet*.

The impulse to begin the poems, as Rilke wrote to
Marlise Gerding in May 1911, came after a period during
which he received what he called "inner dictations,"
words that came to him mornings and evenings and that
struck him with their force and persistence. The process
of writing, as Rilke told Gerding, strengthened and stimu-
lated the inspiration, and he realized that a genuine work
had been initiated.

But the poems that came forth—like the poems that
were to follow in 1901 and 1903—were not intended for
the public. Intimate, sacred to him (Rilke called them
Gebete, prayers), unmentioned in his letters and even in his

journal, these were placed only in the hands of his beloved Lou Andreas-Salomé. *"Gelegt in die Hände von Lou,"* he wrote in dedication when preparing the final manuscript. He chose the title then, inspired by the French medieval tradition of *livres d'heures*, devotional breviaries for lay use.

RILKE'S EARLY LIFE

The poet was born on December 4, 1875, in Prague, then a provincial capital in the Austro-Hungarian Empire, and christened René Karl Wilhelm Johann Josef Maria Rilke. His parents' limited means made them all the more conscious of their social status as members of Prague's small German-speaking elite. In their pretentious, insular world he had, he said, "an anxious, heavy childhood."

An only child, René endured the sentimental upbringing of a mother who still grieved the loss of her baby daughter, and who brought him up as a girl until he was six years old. Increasingly unhappy in her marriage, she took him into churches to pray with her and, as he would later recall with distaste, kiss Christ's wounds on the crucifix. At home she spent long private hours playing with him and dressing him "like a big doll." His father, a stiff, uncommunicative man, was a railroad official who had served as a cadet in the emperor's army, and *he* still grieved the loss of his military career. For his son, the elder Rilke mandated military school.

At ten years old, in prescribed uniform and haircut, René found himself abandoned to an emotionally repressive, loudly regulated, hypermasculine world. He cooperated as well as he could, but his five years there were hateful to him. (Even thirty years later, he would characterize that experience as carrying for him "the feeling of one single terrible damnation.") Teased by the other boys, he was agonizingly lonely, but the cruelest thing was the crowding of the mind in the close quarters, with constantly interrupting commands, bullying, and competition—from which he found relief only in the relative silence and solitude of the infirmary.

Poetry was a refuge for him there, and when ill health finally won him his release from the military academy, poetry shaped the student life into which he threw himself, in Linz and especially in Prague and Munich. Rilke's energy and versatility brought him friends and recognition in university literary circles. Something of a dandy, with his silver-headed cane and bowler hat, he found himself gifted with a strong capacity for relationship, particularly with women, and eager for the discoveries and disclosures these relationships allowed. He adopted easily the romantic lyricism of his time, with its affectations and vaunting, facile subjectivity. Afire with creativity and enthusiastic about his own work, he was tireless in promoting it: not only with famous poets and writers of the period, whom he deluged with letters, but also with the populace at large, among whom he distributed a self-published journal free of charge.

Despite family pressures and expectations, Rilke knew he could not define his life other than as writer, as poet. Yet he was faced with the need to support himself economically, so this calling was hard to defend. He went through the motions of matriculating for a law degree, then for one in philosophy, but the urge to create, to bring to birth something new and necessary, made it impossible to follow through with anything resembling a conventional career. Without support from his family, he turned to others for the material help he needed in order to write, and took up what would become a lifelong burden: seeking a sponsor, an advance on future work, a suitable place to write, a grant or job to tide him through, over and over again explaining, justifying, promising, thanking. Already, however, he was able to point to considerable literary output, as poems, prose pieces, and plays appeared in journals and even on the stage.

The mature Rilke would dismiss the literary efforts of these early years. They surely served his poetic gifts by exercising them, but they embarrassed him later with their shallowness and their essentially imitative character. The soon-to-be-composed *Book of Hours*, although uncharacteristically kept secret for years, was the first work that the poet would acknowledge throughout his life as an authentic expression of his art and his being.

While a student in Munich in 1897, far away from his mother's devout superstitions, René Rilke was drawn to sort through his own religious assumptions and attitudes. He sensed that there must be an authentic ground to the imposing superstructures of his culture's faith, and in a deeply inward process that contrasted with his busy life in coffeehouses, literary salons, and editorial offices, he wanted to find it.

A long series of poems titled *Visions of Christ* presented a superfluous Jesus defeated and shamed by his arrogant attempt to interpose himself between humanity and God. These poems were not published until after Rilke's death, but he did send some to a writer he had not met, who had written an essay that he felt reflected a similar orientation. The essay was "Jesus the Jew," and the writer was Lou Andreas-Salomé.

A two-month sojourn in Tuscany drew Rilke into the world of Italian Renaissance religious art. Avidly he drank it in, exhilarated by the sensuous colors and forms, and the warmly human portrayal of the divine. The unmannered tenderness of Fra Angelico and Botticelli conveyed an authentic, alluring devotion, and showed Rilke that the holy can be rooted in the body and in human relationship.

Lou Andreas-Salomé was a beautiful thirty-six-year-old Russian woman of strong intellect and independent character, born in St. Petersburg and living in a friendly, platonic marriage with an older German professor. When Rilke, at twenty-one, finally met her in a Munich salon in May 1897, she was already noted for Nietzsche's earlier devotion to her. The young poet immediately pursued her with great determination, and they became lovers, in the most passionately fulfilling relationship either had yet known. Lou was the one woman Rilke would never cease loving, while he remained for her, as she later wrote, "the first true reality" in her life; they were "like brother and sister, but from primeval times before incest became a sacrilege." Their friendship, even after it stopped being sexual (at her discretion), was fundamental and generative to every aspect of the poet's development.

To begin with, he quieted down. His energies, scattered centrifugally in the frenzied, somewhat superficial life he had been leading, settled and deepened. Lou's own love of nature pulled him out of the city, out to walk barefoot through meadows and copses that now were real to him in their own right and not just a backdrop to his moods. Lou was at work on a book about Nietzsche, and the iconoclastic philosopher's thought provided a broader context for Rilke's own rebellion against the hypocrisies of conventional Christianity. Two changes in his life were emblematic of Lou's impact: he dropped, at her urging, the name René for the more masculine-sounding Germanic Rainer; and his handwriting was transformed into a more confident, elegant, and relaxed script.

In the spring of 1899, Rilke accompanied Lou and her husband to Russia and discovered the land and the spirituality that would so strongly imbue *The Book of Hours*—and his life. From there, he wrote his friend Frieda von Bülow:

> At bottom one seeks in everything new (country or person or thing) only an expression that helps some personal confession to greater power and maturity. All things are there in order that they may . . . become images for us. And they do not suffer from it, for while they are expressing us more and more clearly, our souls close over them in the same measure. And I feel in these days that Russian things will give me the names for those most timid devoutnesses of my nature which, since my childhood, have been longing to enter my art.

It is as though Rilke had been waiting for whatever in the world would correspond to feeling-states that had been constellating inside him, and he found it in Russia—in the living forms of communal worship he witnessed there, and also in landscape and architecture. He felt in its everyday life a closeness to instinct and passion, which had not survived in the wan and sickened cities of Western Europe. On his return, Rilke tried to keep as much of Russia about him as he could. He launched into a study of Russian literature and went about dressed in Russian peasant garb. When, on September 20, 1899, in Schmargendorf near Berlin, he sat down to write the phrases that spoke themselves within him, it was in the persona of a Russian monk living in a cloister, summoned by the bell to the task of seeing and meeting what was most real to him in the world.

The sixty-seven poems Rilke wrote over the next twenty-five days would form the first part of *The Book of Hours*, called *The Book of a Monastic Life*. These intensely inward conversations with God distilled the seeking of the past years for an unmediated and intimate encounter with the heart of the universe. In November he wrote in his journal—the journal in which he never mentioned *The Book of Hours*—"I have begun my life."

It is possible to read *The Book of Hours* as a cycle of love poems, and it is certainly possible to read into their creation the sensuous awakening of Rilke's relationship with Lou. The God of these poems is a God whom Rilke seeks to love and be possessed by with the same passion he has for Lou, and also with the same passion he has for his vocation.

In the summer of 1900, after another and longer Russian sojourn with Lou, Rilke was invited to Worpswede, an artists' colony in the open heath country near Bremen, which was to play a significant role in his life and imagination. Rilke had been urged by Lou toward greater independence from her, and he felt free to develop new relationships. There he met Clara Westhoff, a gifted and ardent sculptor three years younger than he. She became pregnant, and they were married on April 28, 1901, at her parents' home, and set up housekeeping in a small cottage in Westerwede. There, as the young couple awaited the birth of their child (a daughter, Ruth, born on December 12), thirty-four poems which were to become the second part of *The Book of Hours*—to be named *The Book of Pilgrimage*—came to Rilke. He wrote them in one week, between September 18 and 25.

As the conversations with God are resumed, *The Book of Pilgrimage* reflects Rilke's acute awareness of humanity's unfolding fate as well as his more personal preoccupations. Images of pregnancy enter the religious discourse: God is described as womb, and more frequently as the new life growing inside the poet.

I wish sometimes that you were back inside me,
in this darkness that grew you.   II, 4

Impending fatherhood must have aroused old anger toward the poet's own father. The patriarchal God is rejected now with a vehemence that never occurs in *The Book of a Monastic Life*.

His caring is a nightmare to us,
and his voice a stone.   II, 6

Rilke was facing the task of supporting his young family with almost no material resources and no regular employment. His letters that autumn express a pervasive economic anxiety. Usually such insecurity narrows the focus of one's concern; the wonder is that for the poet the opposite happened, and his heart blew open to the suffering of all humanity. Though Rilke reminds God that

> I'm still the one who knelt before you
> in monk's robes,   II, 2

the persona here is more concerned with the world. The pilgrimage on which he finds himself unites him with that world in the depth of his being.

In August 1902, Rilke went to Paris, commissioned to write a monograph on the sculptor Auguste Rodin. He and Clara had decided to change their life and—leaving Ruth predominantly in the care of her maternal grandparents in their comfortable country home—freed each other to pursue their art. Engaged by Rodin as his secretary, Rilke worked long, demanding hours. He was inspired by the sculptor's relentless self-discipline and re-dedicated himself to the task of poetry with an enhanced respect for craft. But between the demands the great sculptor made on him and his own intense distress over the urban poverty and suffering he beheld in the city around him, Rilke was rarely able to find time or courage for his own work.

In late March 1903, Rilke boarded a train, traveled through the Alpine tunnels to Italy, and took a room at a gardened *pensione* by the sea in Viareggio, which he had loved on his earlier trip. As he wrote to Franz Kappus, to whom the *Letters to a Young Poet* were addressed, he was there to recover from a great physical and moral lassitude. And there, between April 13 and 20, he composed the poems—again thirty-four of them—that make up *The Book of Poverty and Death*, the third in *The Book of Hours*.

Here both death and poverty, viewed so negatively by modern society as evils to flee, are upheld as sources of value and revelation. Instead of canceling life, death is its fruit—and an expression of our most intimate and unique strivings for meaning. This affirmation is all the more poignant in that Rilke had just been warned—by the person he trusted most—of his alleged suicidal tendencies. Apparently he did not resent Lou for making this gratuitous diagnosis at the time of his marriage to Clara, nor was he undone by it; instead he turned death itself into a long-term ally to accompany his life.

The horrors of urban poverty had confronted Rilke in Paris, as he described to Lou in July 1903:

One goes through smells as through many sad rooms. . . . And what people I met . . . almost every day: fragments of caryatids on whom the whole pain still lay, the entire structure of pain, under which they were living, slow as tortoises . . . and under the foot of each day that trod on them, they were enduring like tough beetles . . . twitching like

bits of a big chopped-up fish that is already rotting
but still alive. . . . Oh what kind of a world is that!
Pieces, pieces of people, parts of animals, leftovers
of things that have been, and everything still agi-
tated, as though driven about helter-skelter in an
eerie wind, carried and carrying, falling and over-
taking each other as they fall.

The "poverty poems" of this third book reflect Rilke's
anguish in Paris, and are chillingly close to the life in cities
today. Rilke has been criticized for sentimentalizing
poverty—

Look at them standing about—
like wildflowers, which have nowhere else to grow

III, 19

yet mainly he was simply trying to take it in, that people
can make one another suffer so. He tried to look at the
destitute with the same tender attention that he would
give to a tree. Rilke was not writing deliberately to effect
social change, as was Émile Zola, for instance; he was
doing what from the dictates of his own spiritual integrity
was necessary for any social transformation. That is the
assertion of our essential interconnectedness with each
other and with everything that lives. This is not a political
tenet as much as a profound experience in the core of one's
being. In that sense these poems arise from the same

mystical oneness (we can call it the body of Christ, Anima Mundi, Buddha nature) that pervaded the two earlier books.

RILKE'S LATER LIFE AND WORK
AND ITS RELATIONSHIP TO
THE BOOK OF HOURS

Even before *The Book of Poverty and Death*, Rilke had begun writing the poems that would be included in *The Book of Images*, in a voice more secular and detached than that of *The Book of Hours*. The poems that followed, collected as *New Poems* (*Neue Gedichte*), cast the focus on the thing observed, away from the observer's inner experience. The next two decades of Rilke's development were shaped by an increasing awareness of his role as artist. This self-consciousness replaced the naked, transparent approach to things that characterizes *The Book of Hours*. The capacity to shed his ever more burdensome self-image as poet was not available to him again until February 1922. Then, in a period of less than a month, taken by a trancelike inspiration much like that which had produced *The Book of a Monastic Life*, Rilke composed all fifty-nine *Sonnets to Orpheus* and completed the *Duino Elegies*, begun ten years earlier.

Rilke's life throughout those intervening years 1903 to

1922 had been a pilgrimage in the service—not to say on the surface—of poetry. They had been difficult years of struggle for material survival, restless years of repeated moves from one place to another. Rilke was bedeviled by his dependence on the generosity of benefactors, yet he could not give himself to any work save writing. "It is my old inadequacy," he wrote to Clara. "I have only a single energy which cannot be dispersed." These were years, too, of repeated liaisons, intense involvements that shattered ever again on the rocks of his necessary solitude. Each time Rilke fell in love, he confronted his fear of being sidetracked and consumed. Although he maintained a voluminous correspondence, he lived by himself, refusing even the companionship of animals.

As the years went on, his search for the sacred was supplanted by a tendency to see in everything he encountered "a challenge, a task, a claim to artistic transformation." It is not that Rilke lost his hunger for God; rather, it became transmuted into a single-pointed dedication to art that absorbed into itself everything else in his life. Never again, after *The Book of Hours*, would the dynamic between God and the world be expressed in such immediate and reciprocal terms.

In 1912, ill and depressed and moored in a spell of aridity, Rilke was staying alone at Duino Castle near Trieste, the guest of Princess Maria von Thurn und Taxis. There, one morning, the first lines of the *Duino Elegies* came to him—by divine inspiration, as he later told the princess. Within weeks he had completed the first two elegies; but after that, although he knew there was more to come, Rilke was unable to write the rest. He wandered, frustrated, agitated, in search of circumstances hospitable to his work. In a Europe gearing up for the First World War, Rilke's inner turbulence found no place to be assuaged. More travels, more illness, more troubled relationships; a little work on the *Elegies* now and again; a good deal of public acclaim. But inwardly a lack of vitality plagued Rilke, and bitterness at the violence and nationalism that interfered with his work. In December 1917, he wrote in response to a letter from an admirer of *The Book of Hours*: "I'm not living my own life. . . . I feel refuted, abandoned, and above all threatened by a world ready to dissolve entire in such senseless disorder."

When he was at last able to pick up the thread of the *Elegies*, the spirit from which he wrote was deeply reminiscent of the one that had produced *The Book of Hours*. As he was to write in 1925 to Witold von Hulewicz, his Polish translator, Rilke regarded the *Elegies* as "a further shaping of those essential [inspirations] which had been given already in *The Book of Hours*."

Rilke never repudiated *The Book of Hours*. He maintained that a substantial continuity existed between it and all subsequent works. What had changed most between the inspiration of 1899 and that of 1922 was the almost exclusive stress he put on the function of poetry itself. In the old dialectic equation between person and God, the role of the human became emphasized to the point of isolation—

> If I cried out, who would hear me
> among the hierarchies of angels?

—and that at a most terrifying juncture of history.

Yet still Rilke knew how to sing, and with a singleness of heart, as if the world depended on it:

> . . . Perhaps we are *here* in order to say: house,
> bridge, fountain, gate, pitcher, fruit-tree, window
> .   .   .   .
> . . . And these Things,
> which live by perishing, know you are praising them;
>   transient,
> they look to us for deliverance: us, the most
>   transient of all.

As he wrote these lines of the beloved ninth *Duino Elegy*, the younger Rilke must have taken hold—the one who in 1899 had told God:

> . . . I want to portray you
> not with lapis or gold, but with colors made of apple
>   bark. . . .
> I want, then, simply
> to say the names of things.   I, 60

32

and:

> I would describe myself
> like a landscape I've studied
> at length, in detail;
> like a word I'm coming to understand;
> like a pitcher I pour from at mealtime;
> like my mother's face;
> like a ship that carried me
> when the waters raged.   I, 13

Rilke never lost his conviction in the utter reality of the world, or in our human capacity to redeem it through that act of transforming attention, which is naming—or love.

NOTES

p. 23, "At bottom": Letters of Rainer Maria Rilke 1892–1910, trans. J. B. Greene and M. D. Herter Norton. New York: W. W. Norton, 1945.

p. 24, "I have begun": Tagebücher aus der Frühzeit. Frankfurt: Insel Verlag, 1942.

p. 27, "One goes through": Letters, trans. Greene and Norton.

p. 31, "I'm not living": Cited in introduction to *The Book of Hours,* trans. A. L. Peck. London: Hogarth Press, 1961.

p. 31, "a further shaping": Cited in introduction to *The Book of Hours,* trans. Peck; we changed Peck's "conditions" to "inspirations" for clarity.

p. 32, ". . . Perhaps we are": The Selected Poetry of Rainer Maria Rilke, ed. and trans. Stephen Mitchell. New York: Random House, 1982.

NOTES ON THE TRANSLATION

The relationship between this work and those who have worked on it has been reciprocal. In submitting ourselves to these poems over a period of two and a half years, each of us has been nurtured by them; thus, in successive revisions, we have been able to make changes in part effected by the changes the poems themselves have effected in us. Translation, as George Steiner points out, is, among other things, a work of self-denial, demanding that the translator serve the original rather than impose herself on it. However, as Steiner also points out, all translation—like all reading and even all listening—is a work of editing, a work of interpretation, determined by subjective and contextual factors. What you have in your hands, then, is a translation done by two women in northern California in the 1990s, each with a particular set of experiences that she brought to her understanding of Rilke. Because our translation differs significantly from other translations of these poems, we will point out the kinds of decisions we made concerning form, sound, and substance.

Rilke wrote the poems of *The Book of Hours* in rhymed,

metered verse. In many cases the rhyme scheme was ABAB and the rhythm iambic quatrameter (although Rilke did vary somewhat, e.g., ABAABAB; pentameter rhythms), forms which today sound too singsong to convey accurately the seriousness of Rilke's meaning. In addition, the opening of form in American poetry, particularly since the beginning of this century, reflects the uncertainty and ambiguities of this modern age.

The question, then, of how to be faithful to the musicality of Rilke's poetry without imitating his technique has challenged us through the course of our work. We have chosen to adopt certain of his technical devices—alliteration, the repetition of certain sounds and internal rhymes, for instance—in order to give the reader without German some intimation of the beauty of the original. Here are some examples to show how we worked. We believe that the sound achieved here is a result of our working aloud together.

At some points, in order to lend the English some echo of the rhyme in the original, we chose assonance over outright duplication of the sound—a standard device known as slant rhyme.

Dich wundert nicht des Sturmes Wucht
du hast ihn wachsen sehn:
die Bäume fluchten. Ihre flucht
schafft schreitende Alleen.   II, 1

You are not surprised at the force of the storm—
you have seen it growing.
The trees flee. Their flight
sets the boulevards streaming.

Another example:

Ich bin dein Krug (wenn ich zerscherbe?)
Ich bin dein Trank (wenn ich verderbe?)   I, 36

I am your pitcher (when I shatter?)
I am your drink (when I go bitter?)

We also, in some cases, achieved an internal rhyme reso-
nant with Rilke's:

Nirgends will ich gebogen bleiben,
denn dort bin ich gelogen, wo ich gebogen bin.   I, 13

we translated:

I want to unfold.
Let no place in me hold itself closed,
for where I am closed, I am false.

Rilke makes ample use of alliteration, which, at times,
we were able to render directly into English, given the
similarities between the languages.

Und ich seh dich in meinen Gesichten mit Winden,
    Wassern, und Wäldern
rauschend am Rande des Christentums   I, 60

becomes:

But now I see you:
wind, woods, and water,
roaring at the rim of Christendom.

Or:

Ihr vielen unbestürmten Städte   I, 49

is rendered as:

You many unassaulted cities.

In instances where the rhythm of the original felt appropriate to render in English, we did so. For example, the strong first syllables of I, 19,

Ich bin, du Ängstlicher,

we translated:

I am, you anxious one,

which scans precisely as the German. In other instances, such as II, 25,

Alles wird wieder gross sein und gewaltig,

while we could not imitate the rhythm of the original, we wanted to match the rather exuberant major key of the German (which marks a shift in tone from the poems preceding it) with a rhythm in English auspicious enough to make the shift evident. Thus we chose the heavy, drum-like beat

All will come again into its strength.

We sought always to retain Rilke's naked simplicity, while staying faithful to the subtlety of thought. This led at times to our choosing an English word that, although not literally present in the German, conveyed more concisely the spirit of the original.

Ich bin die Welt,
aus der er irrend fiel   I, 35

would translate literally: "I am the world out of which he, erring, fell." We translated this at first: "I am the world that he fell out of." But on revision we realized that "fell" carried the connotation of Lucifer's fall, and not the sense of mistakenness. Another verb occurred to us, and thus, "I am the world / he stumbled out of," as a way of holding both meanings, fall and error, and of retaining the brevity of the original.

In a similar vein, we chose at times to be faithful to the metaphoric, rather than the literal, meaning of the text, where the literal in English was clumsy or even absurd. In I, 59, for instance, God says, "*Gib mir Gewand*," literally "Give me clothing." We translated this, "Embody me," to convey the task we are to perform for God in the world. In I, 3,

> Doch wie ich mich auch in mich selber neige:
> Mein Gott ist dunkel und wie ein Gewebe

is literally:

> Yet as I also lean into myself:
> My God is dark and like a web.

We translated:

> But when I lean over the chasm of myself
> it seems
> my God is dark
> and like a web.

"Chasm," an image invoked several times in *The Book of Hours*, conveys the contrast Rilke makes in this poem between himself and his more confident and conventional brothers. J. B. Leishman's translation of this line is: "How, though, into myself I keep inclining!" (Leishman's exclamation point).

The above lines indicate the liberties we sometimes took with spacing. In contrast to much American poetry of the past few decades, *The Book of Hours* relies mostly on end-stopped lines, which break at more or less obvious units of thought. Translating for our own time, we often changed the more classic line breaks in order to reflect the open and groping nature of Rilke's thought. Frequently, however, as we reworked the poems, we broke the lines in a manner more consistent with the original.

A major decision, of course, involved which poems and which parts of poems to translate. Of the one hundred thirty-five poems of *Das Stundenbuch* we have translated eighty. We omitted some lines and even entire sections of poems, and collapsed two consecutive poems into one. We have noted such changes in our commentary, and stated our reasons for making them.

Our many omissions were made out of respect for Rilke, to convey and preserve what we considered his essential meaning, undistracted by clichés and undiluted by mixed metaphors. Subtleties of tone translate awkwardly across time and culture; what seemed appropriate to Rilke in Europe nearly a hundred years ago sometimes smacks of pious sentimentality to the American reader on the edge of the twenty-first century. At times the poems start out strong, then dwindle in energy and coherence. That is certainly understandable, when one considers the speed at which Rilke wrote: the sixty-seven poems of the first book were written in three weeks; the thirty-four of the second book in a week; and the thirty-four of the third book likewise. Since we could not bring him the chicken soup he needed on those long nights, we have done him the favor of culling.

These poems were translated in our homes in Berkeley and on several brief retreats in Inverness and Philo, California. Some of them were translated in bright sunshine overlooking Tomales Bay (from suite 11 at the Golden Hinde). Most were translated indoors, on weekday evenings, after both of us had done the work of the day, fed our families, answered mail and phone calls. They were translated at a time of crisis in our world, with survival of life on our planet more and more questionable. Translated as they were in the midst of our lives, encircled by many other kinds of work and commitment, the poems became for each of us an island of "unfraughtness"—as we came to call it—both in their content and in our process. Our work took us beyond the scope of our busy lives, and yet— like a deep-flowing underground stream—it related to and nourished all the rest.

As we collaborated, we developed both a way of working and a more profound understanding of *The Book of Hours* and its individual poems. The effort—including our commentary, introduction, and these notes—has been wholly collaborative. We translated aloud, reading the German, talking about it, then suggesting English wording to each other. Because of this, it is impossible to attribute any aspect of any of the poems to one or the other of us. We combined our strengths and our sensibilities to create a single translator's voice.

Though lucid in language, the poems are often very challenging in thought. Because Rilke's theology and imagery can be difficult to fathom, the fact that there were two of us allowed a level of comprehension to emerge that would have eluded either of us alone. This dialogic process helped keep us faithful to the spirit of the original and helped us avoid too arbitrary or idiosyncratic interpretations. Although at times we did share some of our work with family, friends, and students, and remained open to their comments and suggestions, every decision here was made between the two of us, wrestled with until both of us felt comfortable. Our work together gave rise to discussion about our earliest relationships with the sacred, about the ways in which Rilke's God spanned Joanna's Christian origins and Anita's Jewish beginnings.

We feel deep gratitude for Rilke's *Book of Hours*, and for the opportunity to present it in a contemporary English reading. We thank each other, and our partners and children, who supported us in countless ways during the course of our work. Most of all we acknowledge the young man who, standing at the brink of this fearsome century, opened the treasure house of his huge heart. We, who stand at this end, bow to him in humility, love, and gladness. It is a great blessing to live with these poems and to offer them to others.

THE
BOOK
OF A
MONASTIC
LIFE

Da neigt sich die Stunde und rührt mich an

The hour is striking so close above me,
so clear and sharp,
that all my senses ring with it.
I feel it now: there's a power in me
to grasp and give shape to my world.

I know that nothing has ever been real
without my beholding it.
All becoming has needed me.
My looking ripens things
and they come toward me, to meet and be met.

I, 1

Ich lebe mein Leben in wachsenden Ringen

I live my life in widening circles
that reach out across the world.
I may not complete this last one
but I give myself to it.

I circle around God, around the primordial tower.
I've been circling for thousands of years
and I still don't know: am I a falcon,
a storm, or a great song?

I, 2

Ich habe viele Brüder in Sutanen

I have many brothers in the South
who move, handsome in their vestments,
through cloister gardens.
The Madonnas they make are so human,
and I dream often of their Titians,
where God becomes an ardent flame.

But when I lean over the chasm of myself—
it seems
my God is dark
and like a web: a hundred roots
silently drinking.

This is the ferment I grow out of.

More I don't know, because my branches
rest in deep silence, stirred only by the wind.

I, 3

Wir dürfen dich nicht eigenmächtig malen

We must not portray you in king's robes,
you drifting mist that brought forth the morning.

Once again from the old paintboxes
we take the same gold for scepter and crown
that has disguised you through the ages.

Piously we produce our images of you
till they stand around you like a thousand walls.
And when our hearts would simply open,
our fervent hands hide you.

I, 4

Ich liebe meines Wesens Dunkelstunden

I love the dark hours of my being.
My mind deepens into them.
There I can find, as in old letters,
the days of my life, already lived,
and held like a legend, and understood.

Then the knowing comes: I can open
to another life that's wide and timeless.

So I am sometimes like a tree
rustling over a gravesite
and making real the dream
of the one its living roots
embrace:

a dream once lost
among sorrows and songs.

I, 5

Du, Nachbar Gott, wenn ich dich manchesmal

You, God, who live next door—

If at times, through the long night, I trouble you
with my urgent knocking—
this is why: I hear you breathe so seldom.
I know you're all alone in that room.
If you should be thirsty, there's no one
to get you a glass of water.
I wait listening, always. Just give me a sign!
I'm right here.

As it happens, the wall between us
is very thin. Why couldn't a cry
from one of us
break it down? It would crumble
easily,

it would barely make a sound.

I, 6

Wenn es nur einmal so ganz stille wäre

If only for once it were still.
If the *not quite right* and the *why this*
could be muted, and the neighbor's laughter,
and the static my senses make—
if all of it didn't keep me from coming awake—

Then in one vast thousandfold thought
I could think you up to where thinking ends.

I could possess you,
even for the brevity of a smile,
to offer you
to all that lives,
in gladness.

I, 7

Ich lebe grad, da das Jahrhundert geht

I'm living just as the century ends.

A great leaf, that God and you and I
have covered with writing
turns now, overhead, in strange hands.
We feel the sweep of it like a wind.

We see the brightness of a new page
where everything yet can happen.

Unmoved by us, the fates take its measure
and look at one another, saying nothing.

I, 8

Ich lese es heraus aus deinem Wort

I read it here in your very word,
in the story of the gestures
with which your hands cupped themselves
around our becoming—limiting, warm.

You said *live* out loud, and *die* you said lightly,
and over and over again you said *be*.

But before the first death came murder.
A fracture broke across the rings you'd ripened.
A screaming shattered the voices

that had just come together to speak you,
to make of you a bridge
over the chasm of everything.

And what they have stammered ever since
are fragments
of your ancient name.

I, 9

Ich bin nicht. Der Bruder hat mir was getan

(Abel speaks)

I am not. The brother did something to me
that my eyes didn't see.
He veiled the light.
He hid my face with his face.
Now he is alone.
I think he must still exist,
for no one does to him what he did to me.
All have gone the same way:
all are met with his rage,
beside him all are lost.

I sense my older brother lies awake
as if accused.
Night offers itself to me,
not to him.

I, 10

Du Dunkelheit, aus der ich stamme

You, darkness, of whom I am born—

I love you more than the flame
that limits the world
to the circle it illumines
and excludes all the rest.

But the dark embraces everything:
shapes and shadows, creatures and me,
people, nations—just as they are.

It lets me imagine
a great presence stirring beside me.

— I believe in the night.

I, 11

Ich glaube an Alles noch nie Gesagte

I believe in all that has never yet been spoken.
I want to free what waits within me
so that what no one has dared to wish for

may for once spring clear
without my contriving.

If this is arrogant, God, forgive me,
but this is what I need to say.
May what I do flow from me like a river,
no forcing and no holding back,
the way it is with children.

Then in these swelling and ebbing currents,
these deepening tides moving out, returning,
I will sing you as no one ever has,

streaming through widening channels
into the open sea.

I, 12

Ich bin auf der Welt zu allein und doch nicht
   allein genug

I'm too alone in the world, yet not alone enough
to make each hour holy.
I'm too small in the world, yet not small enough
to be simply in your presence, like a thing—
just as it is.

I want to know my own will
and to move with it.
And I want, in the hushed moments
when the nameless draws near,
to be among the wise ones—
or alone.

I want to mirror your immensity.
I want never to be too weak or too old
to bear the heavy, lurching image of you.

I want to unfold.
Let no place in me hold itself closed,
for where I am closed, I am false.
I want to stay clear in your sight.

I would describe myself
like a landscape I've studied
at length, in detail;
like a word I'm coming to understand;
like a pitcher I pour from at mealtime;
like my mother's face;
like a ship that carried me
when the waters raged.

I, 13

Du siehst, ich will viel

You see, I want a lot.
Maybe I want it all:
the darkness of each endless fall,
the shimmering light of each ascent.

So many are alive who don't seem to care.
Casual, easy, they move in the world
as though untouched.

But you take pleasure in the faces
of those who know they thirst.
You cherish those
who grip you for survival.

You are not dead yet, it's not too late
to open your depths by plunging into them
and drink in the life
that reveals itself quietly there.

I, 14

Wir bauen an dir mit zitternden Händen

Our hands shake as we try to construct you,
block on block.
But you, cathedral we dimly perceive—
who can bring you to completion?

What's Rome? It crumbled.
What is the world? We are destroying it
before your towers can taper into spires,
before we can assemble your face
from the piles of mosaic.

Yet sometimes in dreams
I take in your whole expanse,
from its deepest beginnings
up to the rooftop's glittering ridge.

And then I see: it is my mind
that will fashion
and set the last pieces in place.

I, 15

Daraus, daß Einer dich einmal gewollt hat

Because once someone dared
to want you,
I know that we, too, may want you.

When gold is in the mountain
and we've ravaged the depths
till we've given up digging,

it will be brought forth into day
by the river that mines
the silences of stone.

Even when we don't desire it,
God is ripening.

I, 16

Wer seines Lebens viele Widersinne

She who reconciles the ill-matched threads
of her life, and weaves them gratefully
into a single cloth—
it's she who drives the loudmouths from the hall
and clears it for a different celebration

where the one guest is you.
In the softness of evening
it's you she receives.

You are the partner of her loneliness,
the unspeaking center of her monologues.
With each disclosure you encompass more
and she stretches beyond what limits her,
to hold you.

I, 17

Was irren meine Hände in den Pinseln?

Why am I reaching again for the brushes?
When I paint your portrait, God,
nothing happens.

But I can choose to feel you.

At my senses' horizon
you appear hesitantly,
like scattered islands.

Yet standing here, peering out,
I'm all the time seen by you.

The choruses of angels use up all of heaven.
There's no more room for you
in all that glory. You're living
in your very last house.

All creation holds its breath, listening within me,
because, to hear you, I keep silent.

I, 18

65

Ich bin, du Ängstlicher. Hörst du mich nicht

I am, you anxious one.

Don't you sense me, ready to break
into being at your touch?
My murmurings surround you like shadowy wings.
Can't you see me standing before you
cloaked in stillness?
Hasn't my longing ripened in you
from the beginning
as fruit ripens on a branch?

I am the dream you are dreaming.
When you want to awaken, I am that wanting:
I grow strong in the beauty you behold.
And with the silence of stars I enfold
your cities made by time.

I, 19

Wenn ich gewachsen wäre irgendwo

If I had grown in some generous place—
if my hours had opened in ease—
I would make you a lavish banquet.
My hands wouldn't clutch at you like this,
so needy and tight.

Then I'd have dared to squander you,
you Limitless Now.
I'd have tossed you into the ringing air
like a ball that someone leaps for and catches
with hands outstretched.

I would have painted you: not on the wall
but in one broad sweep across heaven.
I'd have portrayed you brashly:

as mountain, as fire, as a wind
howling from the desert's vastness.

I, 21

Ich finde dich in allen diesen Dingen

I find you there in all these things
I care for like a brother.
A seed, you nestle in the smallest of them,
and in the huge ones spread yourself hugely.

Such is the amazing play of the powers:
they give themselves so willingly,
swelling in the roots, thinning as the trunks rise,
and in the high leaves, resurrection.

I, 22

Ich verrinne, ich verrinne

(Voice of a younger brother)

I'm slipping, I'm slipping away
like sand

slipping through fingers. All
my cells

are open, and all
so thirsty. I ache and swell

in a hundred places, but mostly
in the middle of my heart.

I want to die. Leave me alone.
I feel I am almost there—

where the great terror
can dismember me.

I, 23

Ich liebe dich, du sanftestes Gesetz

I love you, gentlest of Ways,
who ripened us as we wrestled with you.

You, the great homesickness we could never shake
    off,
you, the forest that always surrounded us,

you, the song we sang in every silence,
you dark net threading through us,

on the day you made us you created yourself,
and we grew sturdy in your sunlight. . . .

Let your hand rest on the rim of Heaven now
and mutely bear the darkness we bring over you.

I, 25

Das waren Tage Michelangelo's

Once I read in foreign books
of the time of Michelangelo.
That was a man beyond measure—a giant—
who forgot what the immeasurable was.

He was the kind of man who turns
to bring forth the meaning of an age
that wants to end.
He lifts its whole weight
and heaves it into the chasm of his heart.

The anguish and yearning of all those before him
become in his hands raw matter
for him to compress into one great work.

Only God escapes his will—a God
he loves with a high hatred
for being so out of reach.

I, 29

Ich kann nicht glauben, daß der kleine Tod

I cannot believe that little death
whom we busily ignore
should still trouble us so.

I cannot believe he is that powerful.
I'm still alive, I have time to build.
My blood will outlast the rose.

My knowing is deeper than the teasing way
he likes to toy with our fear.
I am the world
he stumbled out of.

Yet each time the slow procession passes
we're afraid to look.
We don't know: is it the same
as before? is it two now? or ten?
or a thousand? more?

We only know
the cold waxen hand
so naked and near
could be our own.

I, 35

Was wirst du tun, Gott, wenn ich sterbe?

What will you do, God, when I die?

I am your pitcher (when I shatter?)
I am your drink (when I go bitter?)
I, your garment; I, your craft.
— Without me what reason have you?

Without me what house
where intimate words await you?
I, velvet sandal that falls from your foot.
I, cloak dropping from your shoulder.

Your gaze, which I welcome now
as it warms my cheek,
will search for me hour after hour
and lie at sunset, spent,
on an empty beach
among unfamiliar stones.

What will you do, God? I am afraid.

I, 36

Du, gestern Knabe, dem die Wirrnis kam

(To the younger brother)

You, yesterday's boy,
to whom confusion came:
Listen, lest you forget who you are.

It was not pleasure you fell into. It was joy.
You were called to be bridegroom,
though the bride coming toward you is your shame.

What chose you is the great desire.
Now all flesh bares itself to you.

On pious images pale cheeks
blush with a strange fire.
——Your senses uncoil like snakes
awakened by the beat of the tambourine.

Then suddenly you're left all alone
with your body that can't love you
and your will that can't save you.

But now, like a whispering in dark streets,
rumors of God run through your dark blood.

I, 38

Dann bete du, wie es dich dieser lehrt

(To that younger brother)

Now pray,
as I who came back from the same confusion
learned to pray.

I returned to paint upon the altars
those old holy forms,
but they shone differently,
fierce in their beauty.

So now my prayer is this:

You, my own deep soul,
trust me. I will not betray you.
My blood is alive with many voices
telling me I am made of longing.

What mystery breaks over me now?
In its shadow I come into life.
For the first time I am alone with you—

— you, my power to feel.

I, 39

Ich habe Hymnen, die ich schweige

I have hymns you haven't heard.

There is an upward soaring
in which I bend close.
You can barely distinguish me
from the things that kneel before me.

They are like sheep, they are grazing.
I am the shepherd on the brow of the hill.
When evening draws them home
I follow after, the dark bridge thudding,

and the vapor rising from their backs
hides my own homecoming.

I, 40

Dein allererstes Wort war: *Licht*

Your first word of all was *light*,
and time began. Then for long you were silent.

Your second word was *man*, and fear began,
which grips us still.

Are you about to speak again?
I don't want your third word.

Sometimes I pray: Please don't talk.
Let all your doing be by gesture only.
Go on writing in faces and stone
what your silence means.

You be our refuge from the wrath
that drove us out of Paradise.

Be our shepherd, but never call us—
we can't bear to know what's ahead.

I, 44

Du kommst und gehst. Die Türen fallen

You come and go. The doors swing closed
ever more gently, almost without a shudder.
Of all who move through the quiet houses,
you are the quietest.

We become so accustomed to you,
we no longer look up
when your shadow falls over the book we are reading
and makes it glow. For all things
sing you: at times
we just hear them more clearly.

Often when I imagine you
your wholeness cascades into many shapes.
You run like a herd of luminous deer
and I am dark, I am forest.

You are a wheel at which I stand,
whose dark spokes sometimes catch me up,
revolve me nearer to the center.
Then all the work I put my hand to
widens from turn to turn.

I, 45

Ihr vielen unbestürmten Städte

You many unassaulted cities:

Have you never yearned for the enemy,
that he might besiege you
for long irresolute years, until

in hopelessness and hunger you receive him?
He extends like the land beyond your walls,
and he knows he can hold out longer.

Look from your balconies:
there he camps. He does not tire
or diminish in size or strength.
He sends no messengers to threaten
or to promise or persuade.

He who will overcome you
is working in silence.

I, 49

Ich komme aus meinen Schwingen heim

I come home from the soaring
in which I lost myself.
I was song, and the refrain which is God
is still roaring in my ears.

Now I am still
and plain:
no more words.

To the others I was like a wind:
I made them shake.
I'd gone very far, as far as the angels,
and high, where light thins into nothing.

But deep in the darkness is God.

I, 50

Du wirst nur mit der Tat erfaßt

Only in our doing can we grasp you.
Only with our hands can we illumine you.
The mind is but a visitor:
it thinks us out of our world.

Each mind fabricates itself.
We sense its limits, for we have made them.
And just when we would flee them, you come
and make of yourself an offering.

I don't want to think a place for you.
Speak to me from everywhere.
Your Gospel can be comprehended
without looking for its source.

When I go toward you
it is with my whole life.

I, 51

84

Mein Leben hat das gleiche Kleid und Haar

My life bedecks itself no differently
from the deathbeds of the ancient czars.
It's only their power I cannot claim.
I keep my own empires in the background
and manage them in silence.

Their prayer is always: Build,
use everything, build, so terror
may be turned to bigness and even beauty.
And, so that others do not see our fear,
let every kneeling and every pious gesture
be overarched with splendor—
domes, dazzling gold and blue.

I, 52

Und Gott befiehlt mir, daß ich schriebe:

And God said to me, Write:

Leave the cruelty to kings.
Without that angel barring the way to love
there would be no bridge for me
into time.

And God said to me, Paint:

Time is the canvas
stretched by my pain:
the wounding of woman,
the brothers' betrayal,
the city's sad bacchanals,
the madness of kings.

And God said to me, Go forth:

For I am king of time.
But to you I am only the shadowy one
who knows with you your loneliness
and sees through your eyes.

He sees through my eyes
in all the ages.

I, 53

Die Dichter haben dich verstreut

The poets have scattered you.
A storm ripped through their stammering.
I want to gather you up again
in a vessel that makes you glad.

I wander in your winds
and bring back everything I find.

The blind man needed you as a cup.
The servant concealed you.
The homeless one held you out as I passed.

You see, I like to look for things.

I, 55

Gott spricht zu jedem nur, eh er ihn macht

God speaks to each of us as he makes us,
then walks with us silently out of the night.

These are the words we dimly hear:

You, sent out beyond your recall,
go to the limits of your longing.
Embody me.

Flare up like flame
and make big shadows I can move in.

Let everything happen to you: beauty and terror.
Just keep going. No feeling is final.
Don't let yourself lose me.

Nearby is the country they call life.
You will know it by its seriousness.

Give me your hand.

I, 59

Ich war bei den ältesten Mönchen, den Malern und Mythenmeldern

I was there with the first mythmakers and monks
who made up your stories, traced your runes.

But now I see you:
wind, woods, and water,
roaring at the rim of Christendom—
you, land,
to be left in darkness.

I want to utter you. I want to portray you
not with lapis or gold, but with colors made of apple
    bark.
There is no image I could invent
that your presence would not eclipse.

I want, then, simply
to say the names of things.
I'll leave aside kings and their lineages,
their deeds and battles.

— For you are the ground.
The ages to you are only seasons.

You look on the near no differently from the far,
and if they've learned to plant you more deeply
or build more grandly upon you,

you barely feel it. You hear
neither sower nor reaper
when their footsteps pass over you.

I, 60

Du dunkelnder Grund, geduldig erträgst du die Mauern

Dear darkening ground,
you've endured so patiently the walls we've built,
perhaps you'll give the cities one more hour

and grant the churches and cloisters two.
And those that labor—maybe you'll let their work
grip them another five hours, or seven,

before you become forest again, and water, and
    widening wilderness
in that hour of inconceivable terror
when you take back your name
from all things.

Just give me a little more time!
I want to love the things
as no one has thought to love them,
until they're real and ripe and worthy of you.

I want only seven days, seven
on which no one has ever written himself—
seven pages of solitude.

There will be a book that includes these pages,
and she who takes it in her hands
will sit staring at it a long time,

until she feels that she is being held
and you are writing.

I, 61

THE
BOOK
OF
PILGRIMAGE

Dich wundert nicht des Sturmes Wucht

You are not surprised at the force of the storm—
you have seen it growing.
The trees flee. Their flight
sets the boulevards streaming. And you know:
he whom they flee is the one
you move toward. All your senses
sing him, as you stand at the window.

The weeks stood still in summer.
The trees' blood rose. Now you feel
it wants to sink back
into the source of everything. You thought
you could trust that power
when you plucked the fruit;
now it becomes a riddle again,
and you again a stranger.

Summer was like your house: you knew
where each thing stood.
Now you must go out into your heart
as onto a vast plain. Now
the immense loneliness begins.

———————

The days go numb, the wind
sucks the world from your senses like withered
    leaves.

Through the empty branches the sky remains.
It is what you have.
Be earth now, and evensong.
Be the ground lying under that sky.
Be modest now, like a thing
ripened until it is real,
so that he who began it all
can feel you when he reaches for you.

II, 1

Ich bete wieder, du Erlauchter

I am praying again, Awesome One.

You hear me again, as words
from the depths of me
rush toward you in the wind.

I've been scattered in pieces,
torn by conflict,
mocked by laughter,
washed down in drink.

In alleyways I sweep myself up
out of garbage and broken glass.
With my half-mouth I stammer you,
who are eternal in your symmetry.
I lift to you my half-hands
in wordless beseeching, that I may find again
the eyes with which I once beheld you.

I am a house gutted by fire
where only the guilty sometimes sleep
before the punishment that devours them
hounds them out into the open.

I am a city by the sea
sinking into a toxic tide.
I am strange to myself, as though someone unknown
had poisoned my mother as she carried me.

It's here in all the pieces of my shame
that now I find myself again.
I yearn to belong to something, to be contained
in an all-embracing mind that sees me
as a single thing.
I yearn to be held
in the great hands of your heart—
oh let them take me now.
Into them I place these fragments, my life,
and you, God—spend them however you want.

II, 2

Ich bin derselbe noch, der kniete

I'm still the one who knelt before you
in monks' robes, patiently waiting.
You filled him as he called you into being—
a voice from a quiet cell
with the world blowing past.
And you are ever again the wave
sweeping through all things.

That's all there is. Only an ocean
where now and again islands appear.
That's all there is: no harps, no angels.
And the one before whom all things bow
is the one without a voice.

Are you, then, the All? and I the separated one
who tumbles and rages?
Am I not the whole? Am I not all things
when I weep, and you the single one, who hears it?

Listen—don't you hear something?
Aren't there voices other than mine?
Is that a storm? I am one also,
whipping the trees to call to you.

Are you distracted from hearing me
by some whining little tune?
That's mine as well—hear mine as well;
it's lonely and unheard.

I'm the one who's been asking you—
it hurts to ask—Who are you?
I am orphaned
each time the sun goes down.
I can feel cast out from everything
and even churches can look like prisons.

That's when I want you—
you knower of my emptiness,
you unspeaking partner to my sorrow—
that's when I need you, God, like food.

Maybe you don't know what the nights are like
for people who can't sleep.
They all feel guilty—
the old man, the young woman, the child.
They're driven through darkness as though
        condemned,
their pale hands writhing; they're twisted
like a pack of frenzied hounds.

What's past lies still ahead,
and the future is finished.

They see not the faintest glimmer of morning
and listen in vain for the cock's crow.
The night is a huge house
where doors torn open by terrified hands
lead into endless corridors, and there's no way out.

God, every night is like that.
Always there are some awake,
who turn, turn, and do not find you.
Don't you hear them blindly treading the dark?
Don't you hear them crying out
as they go farther and farther down?
Surely you hear them weep; for they are weeping.

I seek you, because they are passing
right by my door. Whom should I turn to,
if not the one whose darkness
is darker than night, the only one
who keeps vigil with no candle,
and is not afraid—
the deep one, whose being I trust,
for it breaks through the earth into trees,
and rises,
when I bow my head,
faint as a fragrance
from the soil.

II, 3

Du Ewiger, du hast dich mir gezeigt

Unending one, you've shown yourself to me.

I love you as I would love a son
who long since went from me,
because his fate called him
to a high place
where he could see out
over all things.

I have stayed home like an old man
who no longer understands his son
and knows little of the new things
that concern him now.

I tremble sometimes for your happiness,
that ventures abroad on so many ships.
I wish sometimes that you were back inside me,
in this darkness that grew you.

And when I get confused by time,
I fear you no longer exist—
though I know, the Evangelist
keeps writing about your eternity.

I am the father; but the son is more.
He is all the father was, and what the father was not
grows great in him. He is the future
and the return. He is the womb, he is the sea. . . .

II, 4

Dir ist mein Beten keine Blasphemie

To you my prayers are no blasphemy:
the old books tell me I am related to you
in a thousand ways.

I want to love you.

Does anyone love a father? Doesn't one turn away
as you turned from me, your face hardened,
wanting to escape these empty, helpless hands?
Doesn't one leave a father's worn-out words
to old books that are seldom read?

Is his heart not a watershed
from which one flows away,
toward passion and suffering?

Isn't the father always that which was?
Used-up years with their odd ways of thinking,
outmoded gestures, old-fashioned dress,
pale hands and ashen hair.

And while in his time he may have been a hero,
he is a leaf that, when we grow, falls away.

II, 5

Und seine Sorgfalt ist uns wie ein Alb

His caring is a nightmare to us,
and his voice a stone.

We would like to heed his words,
but we only half hear them.
The big drama between us
makes too much noise
for us to understand each other.

We watch his lips moving,
shaping sounds that die away.
We feel endlessly distant,
though we are endlessly bound by love.
Only when we notice that he is dying
do we know he lived.

That is Father to us. And I—
I should call you Father?
That would open a gulf between us.
You are my son.

I will know you
as one knows his only beloved child,
even when he has become a man,
an aging man.

II, 6

Du bist der Erbe

So God, you are the one
who comes after.

It is sons who inherit,
while fathers die.
Sons stand and bloom.

You are my heir.

II, 9

Und du erbst das Grün

And you inherit the green
of vanished gardens
and the motionless blue of fallen skies,
dew of a thousand dawns, countless summers
the suns sang, and springtimes to break your heart
like a young woman's letters.

You inherit the autumns, folded like festive clothing
in the memories of poets; and all the winters,
like abandoned fields, bequeath you their quietness.
You inherit Venice, Kazan, and Rome;

Florence will be yours, and Pisa's cathedral,
Moscow with bells like memories,
and the Troiska convent, and that monastery
whose maze of tunnels lies swallowed under Kiev's
    gardens.

Sound will be yours, of string and brass and reed,
and sometimes the songs will seem
to come from inside you.

For your sake poets sequester themselves,
gather images to churn the mind,
journey forth, ripening with metaphor,
and all their lives they are so alone. . . .
And painters paint their pictures only
that the world, so transient as you made it,
can be given back to you,
to last forever.

All becomes eternal. See: In the Mona Lisa
some woman has long since ripened like wine,
and the enduring feminine is held there
through all the ages.

Those who create are like you.
They long for the eternal.
They say, Stone, be forever!
And that means: be yours.

And lovers also gather your inheritance.
They are the poets of one brief hour.
They kiss an expressionless mouth into a smile
as if creating it anew, more beautiful.

Awakening desire, they make a place
where pain can enter;
that's how growing happens.
They bring suffering along with their laughter,

and longings that had slept and now awaken
to weep in a stranger's arms.

They let the riddles pile up and then they die
the way animals die, without making sense of it.
But maybe in those who come after,
their green life will ripen;
it's then that you will inherit the love
to which they gave themselves so blindly, as in a
    sleep.

Thus the overflow from things
pours into you.
Just as a fountain's higher basins
spill down like strands of loosened hair
into the lowest vessel,
so streams the fullness into you,
when things and thoughts cannot contain it.

II, 10

Lösch mir die Augen aus: ich kann dich sehen

Extinguish my eyes, I'll go on seeing you.
Seal my ears, I'll go on hearing you.
And without feet I can make my way to you,
without a mouth I can swear your name.

Break off my arms, I'll take hold of you
with my heart as with a hand.
Stop my heart, and my brain will start to beat.
And if you consume my brain with fire,
I'll feel you burn in every drop of my blood.

II, 7

Ich bin nur einer deiner Ganzgeringen

No one lives his life.

Disguised since childhood,
haphazardly assembled
from voices and fears and little pleasures,

we come of age as masks.
Our true face never speaks.

Somewhere there must be storehouses
where all these lives are laid away
like suits of armor or old carriages
or clothes hanging limply on the walls.

Maybe all paths lead there,
to the repository of unlived things.

II, 11

Und doch, obwohl ein jeder von sich strebt

And yet, though we strain
against the deadening grip
of daily necessity,
I sense there is this mystery:

All life is being lived.

Who is living it, then?
Is it the things themselves,
or something waiting inside them,
like an unplayed melody in a flute?

Is it the winds blowing over the waters?
Is it the branches that signal to each other?

Is it flowers
interweaving their fragrances,
or streets, as they wind through time?

Is it the animals, warmly moving,
or the birds, that suddenly rise up?

Who lives it, then? God, are you the one
who is living life?

II, 12

Alle, welche dich suchen, versuchen dich

All who seek you
test you.
And those who find you
bind you to image and gesture.

I would rather sense you
as the earth senses you.
In my ripening
ripens
what you are.

I need from you no tricks
to prove you exist.
Time, I know,
is other than you.

No miracles, please.
Just let your laws
become clearer
from generation to generation.

II, 15

Wenn etwas mir vom Fenster fällt

How surely gravity's law,
strong as an ocean current,
takes hold of even the smallest thing
and pulls it toward the heart of the world.

Each thing—
each stone, blossom, child—
is held in place.
Only we, in our arrogance,
push out beyond what we each belong to
for some empty freedom.

If we surrendered
to earth's intelligence
we could rise up rooted, like trees.

Instead we entangle ourselves
in knots of our own making
and struggle, lonely and confused.

So, like children, we begin again
to learn from the things,

because they are in God's heart;
they have never left him.

This is what the things can teach us:
to fall,
patiently to trust our heaviness.
Even a bird has to do that
before he can fly.

(leaf out)

II, 16

Manchmal steht einer auf beim Abendbrot

Sometimes a man rises from the supper table
and goes outside. And he keeps on going
because somewhere to the east there's a church.
His children bless his name as if he were dead.

Another man stays at home until he dies,
stays with plates and glasses.
So then it is his children who go out
into the world, seeking the church that he forgot.

II, 19

Du bist die Zukunft, großes Morgenrot

You are the future,
the red sky before sunrise
over the fields of time.

You are the cock's crow when night is done,
you are the dew and the bells of matins,
maiden, stranger, mother, death.

You create yourself in ever-changing shapes
that rise from the stuff of our days—
unsung, unmourned, undescribed,
like a forest we never knew.

You are the deep innerness of all things,
the last word that can never be spoken.
To each of us you reveal yourself differently:
to the ship as coastline, to the shore as a ship.

II, 22

Die Könige der Welt sind alt

The kings of the world are old and feeble.
Who are their heirs?

Their sons are dying before they are men,
and their pale daughters
abandon themselves to the brokers of violence.

Their crowns are exchanged for money
and melted down into machines,
and there is no health in it.

Does the ore feel trapped
in coins and gears? In the petty life
imposed upon it
does it feel homesick for earth?

If metal could escape
from coffers and factories,
and the torn-open mountains
close around it again,

we would be whole.

II, 24

Alles wird wieder groß sein und gewaltig

All will come again into its strength:
the fields undivided, the waters undammed,
the trees towering and the walls built low.
And in the valleys, people as strong
and varied as the land.

And no churches where God
is imprisoned and lamented
like a trapped and wounded animal.
The houses welcoming all who knock
and a sense of boundless offering
in all relations, and in you and me.

No yearning for an afterlife, no looking beyond,
no belittling of death,
but only longing for what belongs to us
and serving earth, lest we remain unused.

II, 25

Auch du wirst groß sein. Größer noch als einer

You too will find your strength.
We who must live in this time
cannot imagine how strong you will become—
how strange, how surprising,
yet familiar as yesterday.

We will sense you
like a fragrance from a nearby garden
and watch you move through our days
like a shaft of sunlight in a sickroom.

We will not be herded into churches,
for you are not made by the crowd,
you who meet us in our solitude.

We are cradled close in your hands—
and lavishly flung forth.

II, 26

Es wird nicht Ruhe in den Häusern, sei's

There will be no rest in the houses:

                          the stir

of departure—

                  someone being carried to his grave,
and another, taking up the pilgrim's staff,
to ask in unknown places for the path
where he knows you are waiting.

So many are drawn now to move toward you,
the roads are never empty.
There are so many
we can't make out their faces
or know their names,
and when they finally reach you
they are tired.

I have seen them moving like a tide.
Since then, I think the winds themselves
are stirred by the blowing of their cloaks,
and subside again when they lie down,

so great is their going across the plains.

                                   II, 27

In tiefen Nächten grab ich dich, du Schatz

In deep nights I dig for you like treasure.
For all I have seen
that clutters the surface of my world
is poor and paltry substitute
for the beauty of you
that has not happened yet.

My hands are bloody from digging.
I lift them, hold them open in the wind,
so they can branch like a tree.

Reaching, these hands would pull you out of the sky
as if you had shattered there,
dashed yourself to pieces in some wild impatience.

What is this I feel falling now,
falling on this parched earth,
softly,
like a spring rain?

II, 34

THE
BOOK
OF
POVERTY
AND
DEATH

Vielleicht, daß ich durch schwere Berge gehe

It feels as though I make my way
through massive rock
like a vein of ore
alone, encased.

I am so deep inside it
I can't see the path or any distance:
everything is close
and everything closing in on me
has turned to stone.

Since I still don't know enough about pain,
this terrible darkness makes me small.
If it's you, though—

press down hard on me, break in
that I may know the weight of your hand,
and you, the fullness of my cry.

III, 1

Du Berg, der blieb da die Gebirge kamen

You, mountain, here since mountains began,
slopes where nothing is built, peaks that no one has
    named,
eternal snows littered with stars,
valleys in flower—

Do I move inside you now?
Am I within the rock
like a metal that hasn't been mined?
Your hardness encloses me everywhere.

Or is it fear
I am caught in? The tightening fear
of the swollen cities
in which I suffocate.

III, 2

Denn, Herr, die großen Städte sind

Lord, the great cities are lost and rotting.
Their time is running out.
The people there live harsh and heavy,
crowded together, weary of their own routines.

Beyond them waits and breathes your earth,
but where they are it cannot reach them.

Their children waste their days
on doorsteps, always in the same shadow.
They don't know that somewhere
wind is blowing through a field of flowers.

The young girls have only strangers to parade
    before,
and no one sees them truly;
so, chilled,
they close.

And in back rooms they live out the nagging years
of disappointed motherhood. Their dying is long

---

and hard to finish: hard to surrender
what you never received.

Their exit has no grace or mystery.
It's a little death, hanging dry and measly
like a fruit inside them that never ripened.

III, 4/5

O Herr, gib jedem seinen eignen Tod

God, give us each our own death,
the dying that proceeds
from each of our lives:

the way we loved,
the meanings we made,
our need.

III, 6

Denn wir sind nur die Schale und das Blatt

For we are only the rind and the leaf.

The great death, that each of us carries inside,
is the fruit.

Everything enfolds it.

III, 7

Herr: Wir sind ärmer denn die armen Tiere

Lord, we are more wretched than the animals
who do their deaths once and for all,
for we are never finished with our not dying.

Dying is strange and hard
if it is not our death, but a death
that takes us by storm, when we've ripened none
    within us.

We stand in your garden year after year.
We are trees for yielding a sweet death.
But fearful, we wither before the harvest.

III, 8

Ich will ihn preisen. Wie vor einem Heere

Loud as a trumpet
in the vanguard of an army,
I will run ahead and proclaim.

My words will be sweet to hear.
My people will drink them in like wine
and not get drunk.

And on spring nights, when few remain
around my tent, I will make music as soft
as northern Aprils, that hover,
late and tender, around each leaf.

So my voice becomes both a breath and a shout.
One prepares the way, the other
surrounds my loneliness with angels.

III, 11

Und gib, daß beide Stimmen mich begleiten

May both voices accompany me,
when I am scattered again in city and fear.

They will serve me in the fury of our time
and help me make a place for you

wherever you need to be.

III, 12

Die großen Städte sind nicht wahr; sie täuschen

The big cities are not true; they betray
the day, the night, animals and children.
They lie with silence, they lie with noise
and with all that lets itself be used.

None of the vast events that move around you
happens there. In city streets and alleys
your great winds falter and churn,
and in frenzied traffic grow confused.

III, 13

Denn Gärten sind—von Königen gebaut

These winds—they come to gardens too.

There are gardens made by kings. For a time
they took pleasure there
with maidens who braided
their lovely laughter into garlands.

Like breezes through the leaves
was their whispering to each other.
They glistened in their silks and furs,
and their robes rustled over the gravel paths like
    running water.

They are gone now. And now all gardens
follow after them,
subside in stillness through disenchanted springtimes
and slowly burn in the flames of autumn.

Beyond the gardens still glimmers the palace—
bereft of festivals, paintings fading
in empty halls—silent, patient,
willing to let go.

III, 14

Dann sah ich auch Paläste, welche leben

But the privileged ones today refuse to fade:
they boast of their wealth, yet they are not rich.

Not rich like the nomad chieftains
whose multitudes of sheep
swept across green plains
like a morning tide;
or those whose camels moved against the sky
in majestic silhouettes.

The smell of their cattle herds
lingered, warm and heavy,
ten days after they passed.
And, as at a fine wedding, the good wine
flows the whole night through,
so ran the milk from their she-asses.

And not like the desert sheiks
who slept at night on faded carpets
but had rubies set in silver combs
to groom their favorite mares.

And not like those princes who found
no allurement in gold—no fragrance there—
but anointed their proud lives
with almond oil, amber, and sandalwood.

Those were riches that made life
vast and voluptuous.
Now the days of riches are gone
and no one can call them back for us.

But we can let ourselves be poor again.

III, 15

Sie sind es nicht. Sie sind nur die Nicht-Reichen

We are not poor. We are just without riches,
we who have no will, no world:
marked with the marks of the latest anxiety,
disfigured, stripped of leaves.

Around us swirls the dust of the cities,
the garbage clings to us.
We are shunned as if contaminated,
thrown away like broken pots, like bones,
like last year's calendar.

And yet if our Earth needed to
she could weave us together like roses
and make of us a garland.

For each being is cleaner than washed stones
and endlessly yours, and like an animal
who knows already in its first blind moments
its need for one thing only—

to let ourselves be poor like that—as we truly are.

III, 16

Du bist der Arme, du der Mittellose

You are the poor one, you the destitute.
You are the stone that has no resting place.
You are the diseased one
whom we fear to touch.
Only the wind is yours.

You are poor like the spring rain
that gently caresses the city;
like wishes muttered in a prison cell, without a world
   to hold them;
and like the invalid, turning in his bed to ease the
   pain.
Like flowers along the tracks, shuddering
as the train roars by, and like the hand
that covers our face when we cry—that poor.

Yours is the suffering of birds on freezing nights,
of dogs who go hungry for days.
Yours the long sad waiting of animals
who are locked up and forgotten.

You are the beggar who averts his face,
the homeless person who has given up asking;
you howl in the storm.

III, 18

Du, der du weißt, und dessen weites Wissen

You who know, and whose vast knowing
is born of poverty, abundance of poverty—

make it so the poor are no longer
despised and thrown away.

Look at them standing about—
like wildflowers, which have nowhere else to grow.

III, 19

Betrachte sie und sieh, was ihnen gliche

Look at them and see what they are like:

they move as though a wind were pushing them,
they rest as though a hand had stopped them.

In their eyes is the oncoming darkness
sweeping across summer's fields
before the storm.

III, 20

Denn sieh: sie werden leben und sich mehren

There's also this to see: They will live on, they will
    increase,
no longer pawns of time.
They will grow like the sweet wild berries
the forest ripens as its treasure.

Then blessed are those who never turned away
and blessed are those who stood quietly in the rain.
Theirs shall be the harvest; for them the fruits.

They will outlast the pomp and power
of lawmakers, whose meanings will crumble.
When all else is exhausted and bled of purpose,
they will lift their hands, that have survived.

III, 28

Nur nimm sie wieder aus der Städte Schuld

Only retrieve them from the cities' guilt,
where everything for them is anger and confusion,
and wounded patience sucks them dry.

Has the earth, then, no room for them?
Whom does the wind seek? For whom
is the wet glistening of streams?

Is there by the banks
of the pond's deep dreaming
nowhere they can see their faces reflected?

They need only, as a tree does,
a little space in which to grow.

III, 29

Thanksgiving

So bin ich nur als Kind erwacht

I thank you, deep power
that works me ever more lightly
in ways I can't make out.
The day's labor grows simple now,
and like a holy face
held in my dark hands.

 I, 62

COMMENTARY

I, 1 Our monk's cell seems to be directly under the bell tower.

The thoughts and words that were to go into *The Book of Hours* had been coming to Rilke in the mornings and evenings, as from some inner dictation. These first verses capture much of what will follow. From the start there is the conviction that our presence in the universe is part of a reciprocal process. Things need to be seen in order to be real—and so do we and so will God, whom Rilke does not yet mention here.

The original has a third stanza, which we translated thus:

> No thing is too small for me to cherish
> and paint in gold, as if it were an icon
> that could bless us,
> though I'll not know who else among us
> will feel this blessing.

We omit it only because it is not as strong as the first two stanzas, especially for the opening poem of *The Book of Hours*.

I, 2 Rilke wrote of the circles that they *"sich über die Dinge ziehn,"* literally "draw themselves over the things." Clearly what he intended was the things of this world (see the introduction).

I, 3 On a sojourn in Italy not long before, Rilke had come to love Italian painting, particularly works of the Renaissance. He and Lou Andreas-Salomé were making a study of them. As he wrote to Frieda von Bülow in August 1897: "I am especially fascinated by one Florentine master of the quattrocento—Sandro Botticelli, whom I now want to go into somewhat more deeply and personally. His Madonnas with their weary sadness, their great eyes asking for release and fulfillment . . . stand at the heart of the longing of our time" (*Letters of Rainer Maria Rilke 1892–1910*, trans. J. B. Greene and M. D. Hexter Norton. New York: W. W. Norton, 1945).

I, 4 Despite his love for Italian painting, Rilke was acutely aware of the limitations of any representational art with respect to the sacred.

I, 5 Rilke suggests here that we live in two dimensions at once: our immediate dramas ("sorrows and songs") and the larger context (the over-rustling tree) in which they find meaning.

I, 6 We omitted the last seven lines, which lost the

thread of the preceding image and repeated the thought that is in I, 4. After all, Rilke was writing these very quickly!

I, 7   Here is one of the many instances in *The Book of Hours* where Rilke speaks in a voice in which Eastern and Western spiritual experience converge, where emptiness (Buddhism) and devotion (Christian, and also Hindu and Sufi) come together.

I, 8   This poem, among others, made us want to translate *The Book of Hours* at this moment. What was it in the experience of this twenty-three-year-old man that allowed him such a sinister intuition of what the twentieth century would bring?

I, 9   Rilke is, of course, referring to Cain's murder of his brother Abel.

I, 10   This subtle treatment of the hugeness of our guilt will be taken up again, but differently, when Rilke writes of the poor and oppressed in the third volume of *The Book of Hours*.

I, 12   To avoid excessive piety, we changed Rilke's "*frömmsten Gefühle*" ("most devout feelings") to "what waits within me."

I, 13   In the passage beginning, "I would describe my-self," Rilke reveals a key element of his aesthetic and spiritual path, which is to place himself humbly and grate-fully among the things of this world.

I, 14   The original includes the phrase: *"durch ihres leichten Gerichts / glatte Gefühle gefürstet,"* which has more nuances than we could convey in English. The lines sug-gest that the indifferent glide through life and rise to a princely state as a function of their lack of feeling.

I, 15   Note the juxtaposition between the construction of God, which we can carry out like good craftspeople, and an intuitive knowing. In dreams, our perception of God can be more complete.

I, 16   Creation unfolds as a natural, uncontrollable pro-cess, beyond the reaches of our will. Note the implicit contrasts here, as Rilke uses the most resistant of material elements to convey the operation of grace.

I, 17   Here, instead of deconstructing the gender, as we did in I, 5, we have changed it outright.

I, 18   See I, 36 ("What will you do, God, when I die?") and I, 39 ("you, my power to feel"). In our assiduous pursuit of the divine it is easy to forget that God's aware-ness of us is not contingent on our perception of God.

I, 19 This clearly follows on the previous poem. God is reassuring the one who is peering out anxiously on the beach. As Augustine said, "Thou wouldst not seek me if thou hadst not already found me."

I, 21 We have omitted six lines in the middle of this poem and a dozen at the end, where very different metaphors entered, and in a sentimental fashion.

Later, in *Sonnet to Orpheus* II, 8 (1922), the childhood memory of playing ball will resurface. The ball, instead of being equated with God, as here, will signify life itself. "*What* in the world was real? / Nothing. Only the balls. Their magnificent arches. / Not even the children. . . . But sometimes one, / oh a vanishing one, stepped under the plummeting ball" (*The Selected Poetry of Rainer Maria Rilke*, ed. and trans. Stephen Mitchell. New York: Random House, 1982).

I, 22 It is through seeing and cherishing things that Rilke resacralizes the world. "Things" includes not only artifacts, but also organic beings, such as trees, which—in Rilke's work as in Buddhism—bear meanings of wisdom as well as fertility. A passage from a letter Rilke wrote to Ilse Jahr in 1922 elucidates the importance of this in *The Book of Hours*, and the relationships he understood among things and God and community:

"I began with things, which were the true confidants of my lonely childhood. . . . Then Russia opened itself to me and granted me the brotherliness and the darkness of God, in whom alone there is community. That was what I *named* him then, the God who had broken in upon me, and for a long time I lived in the antechamber of his name, on my knees" (*Selected Poetry*, ed. and trans. Mitchell).

I, 23   Here Rilke redeems "negative" mind states such as fear (just as he will do shortly with lust). In this he reveals a capacity for tantric play, unusual in a nineteenth-century Western man.

I, 25   Notice how little Rilke whines. He evokes our alienation and imminent decline without one sour self-pitying note.

I, 29   Rilke can love what he sees as outdated without disparaging it. He can turn and view with tenderness even our arrogance.

I, 35   Here the movement of feelings regarding death, from casual unconcern to naked fear, is similar to the movement in the German medieval mystery play *Jedermann* (*Everyman*).

I, 36   Continuing from the previous poem, circling around death, Rilke comes upon a more poignant loss. It is the loss of a relationship that is already larger than our own life.

See the comment for I, 18: We exist in part to give God something to gaze upon tenderly. Our vulnerable relationship to God is more important to Rilke than God's objective existence. As he wrote in a letter to his friend Mimi Romanelli in 1910:

"How far I feel this morning from the misers who, before they pray, demand to know if God exists. If he no longer exists or does not yet exist, what does it matter? It will be my prayer that will create him, for it is pure creation as it soars to the skies. And if the God my prayer projects does not persist, that's just as well: we'll make him afresh, he'll be less used up" (*Briefe*, vol. 1, *1897–1914*. Wiesbaden: Insel Verlag, 1950).

I, 38   Here, with an audacity which—for his time—is stunning, Rilke places the erotic in service to the sacred.

I, 39   As with Hindu and Sufi devotionalism, the erotic is revealed here as inseparable from our longing for God.

We omitted six lines, in which the soul is excessively and distastefully feminized.

I, 40   Rilke foresaw not only the apocalyptic times that have fallen upon us, but also our denial of them.

I, 45   God moves through us, as though we were doors or houses or city streets (I, 38) or forests. We, like all things, are continually being interpenetrated by God.

I, 49   This reminds us of John Donne's *Holy Sonnet* that begins: "Batter my heart, three-person'd God," and goes on to say: "I, like an usurpt town . . . / Take me to you, imprison me, for I / Except you enthrall me, never shall be free." There is a sense of fated surrender, and a deeply erotic tension.

I, 50   Twenty-eight lines follow, which we have omitted. Taking our cue from line 7, we decided to translate no more words here.

I, 51   To a degree unusual for a Westerner, Rilke sees simultaneously the world-generating power of mind and its inherent limitations. Rilke already intuited that the spiritual journey appropriate to the twentieth century is, as Jung asserted, a journey not toward perfection, but toward wholeness.

I, 52   We omitted the final stanza (five lines) because the thread was lost.

Rilke had beheld the dazzling onion domes of the czars only months before, on his first epochal journey to Russia.

I, 53   Did the poet hear these words in Schmargendorf in the early autumn of 1899, when the poems of *The Book of Hours* first began pouring out of him?

Rilke here turns obstacle into opportunity. He can hold together the utterly transcendent and the immanent—the God of greatest glory and the lost, forsaken one within.

See the eighth *Duino Elegy* for Rilke's moving treatment of time and timelessness, where human boundedness in time is contrasted with the natural world's freer acceptance: "And where we see the future, it sees all time / and itself within all time, forever healed" (*Selected Poetry*, ed. and trans. Mitchell).

I, 55 We have omitted eight lines that didn't fit in the cup.

It wasn't just the first murder that fragmented God's ancient names (see I, 9), but also our presumptuous attempts to describe God. From the *Tao Te Ching*: "The Way that can be named is not the Way."

I, 59 This poem provides our preferred marching orders for the twenty-first century. Note the reciprocity of caring as we embody God and God guides us by the hand. The German echoes this relationship in the rhyme and rhythm of *"Gib mir Gewand"* (which literally means "Give me clothing," and which we have translated "Embody me") and *"Gib mir die Hand,"* "Give me your hand."

I, 60 See the passage we quote from the ninth *Duino Elegy* in our introduction, and our comments on it. This poem marks a shift in *The Book of Hours*, where in Rilke's ever-deepening perception of God's immensity and of the sacredness of embodiment, God becomes identified with Earth itself.

I, 61   This poem has become an anthem of the deep ecology movement, thanks to Joanna Macy in her workshops and Anita Barrows in her talks on ecopsychology.

To find the book mentioned in the last lines, look in your hands.

II, 1   In spite of the two-year interlude, this opening poem carries right on from the final movement of *The Book of a Monastic Life*. As God is recognized as Earth, so are we, invited to go out into the world as into our own hearts. Similarly, we are urged not only to find sacredness in things, but also to become a thing ourselves, and to ripen until we are real.

Of all the seasons, Rilke most loved autumn. He found it released his creative powers.

II, 2   Already in 1901, Rilke prefigures the broken faces of Picasso, and also the toxic tides and intrauterine contaminations of the century's end.

II, 3   See I, 25, "you dark net threading through us." See also the first words of the *Duino Elegies*: "If I cried out, who would hear me / among the hierarchies of angels?" These more famous lines written in 1922 take up the questioning Rilke is doing in the sixth stanza here.

II, 4   Rilke really did say "inside me": this is not Barrows and Macy reconstructing gender! Rilke sees us all as pregnant with the future, pregnant with God.

II, 5   See the introduction. Rilke wrote these poems while awaiting the birth of his child and while saddled with domestic worries. His sense of alienation from his own father must have been aroused.

II, 6   Rilke was very strongly influenced by Nietzsche, through Lou; but to Rilke it's only the Big Daddy God who is dead.

Rilke's relationship with his own father, an ambitious but failed military man, was a source of great suffering to the poet. Rilke senior had little understanding of his son's life choices, and did not approve of them.

II, 9   Rilke's father died in March 1906, three months after the publication of *The Book of Hours*. What Rilke inherited came not from his parents so much as from Russia and Italy, from Lou and Rodin, from his planet-people's journey through time, from earth and from sky.

II, 10   Here again, the ninth *Duino Elegy* is prefigured (see the introduction).

II, 7   No, this is not a misnumbering. We have altered Rilke's ordering of the poems so as not to interrupt the sequence that immediately precedes and which seems all of a piece. This poem, which was written in 1897, was originally addressed not to God but to Lou. Rilke slipped it under her door in the cottage where they had their first and greatest passionate idyll. Until their publication in 1905, Lou was the only person to whom Rilke showed the poems of *The Book of Hours*.

II, 11 We have omitted the poem's first eight lines because they are less clear and unified than what follows.

Here the images, which recall the museums in Munich, suggest a dying culture. It is from and for this grand outmoded culture that our masks are fashioned.

From Rilke's journal, November 3, 1899: "The sense people have of impermanence and perishing comes mostly from their own not-having-been-ness [*Nicht-gewesen-sein*]. In order to be, it is not enough to be born" (*Tagebücher aus der Frühzeit*. Frankfurt: Insel Verlag, 1942).

II, 12 The shift here in sense of agency—even who the agent is—bespeaks the experience of grace. As in the development of the ecological self, we realize that we are "being lived" by a vaster power and from a deeper source than our skin-encapsulated ego.

II, 15 Again the mystic speaks to the theologian, saying: "Be still and know."

We have translated *Gesetze* as both "Ways" (I, 25) and "laws." Unusual in a mystic is how Rilke appreciates the lawful unfolding of the Way. This is close to the Buddhist meaning of Dharma.

II, 16 Rilke ended with a five-line parenthesis, which we omit. It surrealistically likens angels to penguins who have forgotten how to fly.

II, 19 Soon Rilke, too, would leave the home he had made with his wife and baby daughter in Westerwede. His poetry was at stake; but while he felt forced to flee the narrow confines of domesticity, he maintained a lifelong friendship with Clara Westhoff and loyally promoted her artistic work.

II, 22 We translated *"Inbegriff"* as "innerness"; the literal sense is "inner meaning."

Note how Rilke links the future with the innermost part of our being, like a seed we carry within us. Although Rilke intuits the oncoming darkness and unprecedented suffering the century will bring, he also affirms—and in this there is profound hopefulness—the organic ripening of our true nature.

II, 24 Here Rilke speaks in the great ongoing tradition of poets such as Dante and Neruda who take on the political and economic realities of their time. Rilke conveys the exhaustion of political will and the profound loss of vitality resulting from the growing power of industrial capital.

II, 25   This follows directly on the preceding poem, with a striking shift to a different key. Rilke sees that our freeing ourselves from the power of money does not mean fleeing what is material. We seek not to transcend the things of this world, but to learn to care for them more deeply.

II, 26   Note the dialectic in our relationship with God. Like all mystics, we know the divine through our solitude; yet only in our community can this knowledge grow.

II, 27   Pilgrimage, which furnishes the title to this book, and which was suggested from its first poem, now becomes explicit. Whereas in the poem about the force of the storm (II, 1) we are called into our own vast loneliness, here it is clear that pilgrimage is also a collective endeavor.

The true experience of community is not in staying with the status quo, but in moving forth together, in response to a summons, toward a future that cannot yet be envisioned.

If Rilke were alive today, he probably would see the overwhelming numbers of refugees, and their tidal movements across old political boundaries, in terms of pilgrimage toward a future we cannot yet discern.

II, 34   Perhaps the pilgrimage we are making is not so much to redeem ourselves as to rescue God.

We omitted the middle section of the poem, which brought forward a separate theme:

> But the way to you is terribly far,
> hard to make out, overgrown.
> No one has walked it for a long time.
>
> How lonely you are—
> you are loneliness itself,
> dear heart that drifts into distant valleys.

III, 1   Donald Prater, one of Rilke's many biographers (*A Ringing Glass*. Oxford: Clarendon Press, 1986), says that this poem was prompted by Rilke's claustrophobia in the train tunnels through the Alps on his way to Viareggio.

III, 2   A contemporary note is struck here, as the poet experiences that the distress of urban civilization is something he carries inside him. Here, after the anguish he witnessed in Paris, he speaks already of "the swollen cities."

III, 4/5   We have combined most of 4 with the last three lines of 5. The two themes of this book, poverty and death, emerge at the same time. The tragedy of the urban poor is reflected in their being deprived of even the ground in which to grow a meaningful death.

III, 6   Our living includes our dying.

III, 7   Our living grows our dying organically. These are the first several of seventeen original lines—what we felt to be the core.

III, 8   Again we have harvested the fruit, this time from an original of twenty-eight lines.

III, 11   What Rilke is proclaiming in this first stanza is made clear in the previous two poems, which we have omitted: our human capacity consciously to grow death.

We have spared the reader Rilke's images about men being pregnant.

III, 12   The original this time is actually as brief as our translation. Both these voices are within every one of us; we need to use them now, scattered as we are "in city and fear."

III, 13   Not only are the cities lost (III, 4/5), but within them the very forces of nature become lost as well.

III, 14   The first line here comes at the end of the previous poem. We include it with this one because it announces its theme.

III, 15   We omitted thirteen lines. In this poem is a celebration of sensory wealth rare for a northern European.

III, 16,18,19   Because of the sentiments expressed here, Rilke was sometimes accused of romanticizing poverty. Yet his anguish in beholding the poor was genuine. Describing his experience in Paris, he wrote later to Lou Andreas-Salomé:

"O Lou, I was so tormented day after day. For I understood all those people, and although I went around them in a wide arc, they had no secret from me. I was torn out of myself into their lives, through all their burdened lives" (*Letters*, trans. Greene and Norton).

III, 20   This is another of Rilke's prophetic poems.

III, 28   For Rilke the sense of the future remains strong. No horror of the present can excise the fact that tomorrow will dawn and that change is constant. The lawfulness in nature that he has celebrated in earlier poems here supports his confidence that goodness will not die.

III, 29   The poet's exquisite gratitude for nature is so real that he can extend it now to embrace the lost ones in the doomed cities.

I, 62   This is the last of the poems we translated from *The Book of a Monastic Life*. We placed it here because it provides a simple, gratifying, and integrative closure for the whole work.

The poem begins with twelve lines that we have omitted because of a certain sentimentality. They evoke the childlike constancy of the poet's trust, and his sweet discovery that it returns again and again throughout life.